Baltimore Oriole

Song Sparrow

PVI An imprint of PVIMaine LLC

What's That Bird?
A Kid's Guide to Backyard Birds of New England

By Ingrid J Whitaker & Ethan J Whitaker

Copyright © 2022 by PVIMaine LLC

Library of Congress Cataloging-in-Publication Data

ISBN: 979-8-9856205-4-2 (paperback)
ISBN: 979-8-9856205-5-9 (hardcover)
ISBN: 979-8-9856205-6-6 (kindle)
ISBN: 979-8-9856205-7-3 (epub)

Requests for Information:
Mail: PVIMaine LLC
attn: Ethan Whitaker
117 Cushman Point Rd
Wiscasset, Maine 04578

Phone: 1-207-671-2006

E-Mail: ewhitaker@PVIMaine.com

Table of Contents

Learning Pages

Birds are everywhere, and one of the best things about birding is that you can do it anywhere! All you need is a window or a place to go outside. When you find a bird, a field guide such as this one will help you answer the question, "What's that bird?"

You already know that birds move quickly! They are always busy singing, searching for food, caring for their young or finding shelter. Just like the birds, you must act quickly too! There are a number of things to look at when identifying a bird. How can you do that when birds stay still for a such short amount of time? Here are some tips:

When you first look at the bird, take it all in. Don't focus on one feature too long, or the bird will be gone before you have enough information to bring to a field guide. Take a snapshot in your head noting these features:

Size: Is this one of the larger birds that comes to your feeder, or smaller? How does its size compare to other birds? Is it the size of a chickadee? Is it the size of a robin? Or how about a crow?

In this book, you will see a size scale for each bird. It shows you how this bird's size compares to that of three common birds: the Black-Capped Chickadee, the American Robin, and the American Crow.

Here is an example from the Eastern Bluebird page.

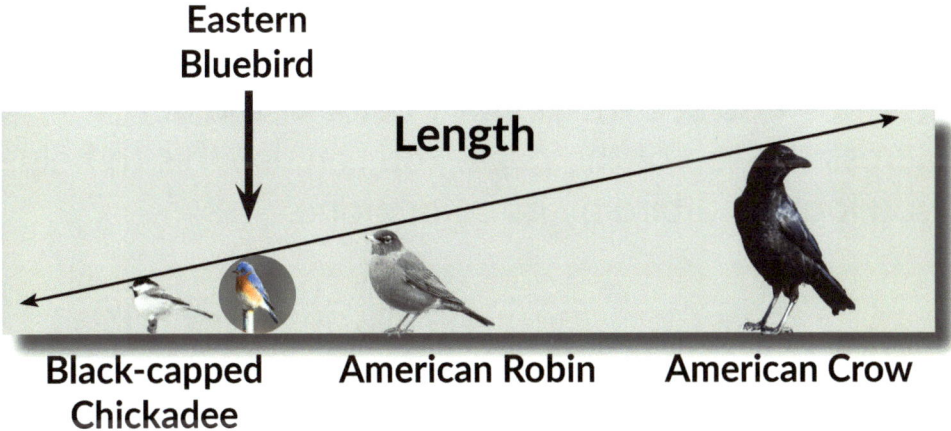

Eastern Bluebird

Length

Black-capped Chickadee   **American Robin**   **American Crow**

Color: What is the primary, or main, color of the bird? Keep in mind that color can vary with the gender of a bird and the time of year. Some birds' plumage, or feathers, change from one season to another. A male goldfinch in breeding plumage (spring and summer), for example, is a bright yellow, but a female or a male

Female

in non-breeding plumage (fall and winter) is a drab tannish brown with just a hint of yellow.

In this book, you will notice that for some birds a picture of the female is included. If there isn't a picture of the female, that means she looks the same as the male.

You will also see the primary color of the bird across the top of the page. You can use this to help you look up a bird by its color alone.

American Goldfinch
Spinus tristis

Yellow
Black
White

If you do not find your bird, or you have it narrowed down to a few but need more information to make a positive identification, look again (and again) at the bird and make note of the following:

Special Markings: Known as 'field marks', these are the unique features of a bird such as markings on the wing – does it have white or dark bars?, the chest – is it streaked or spotted?, tail – are there colored tips or streaks?, the head – is there a colored spot on the crown (top) or back of the head? Are there lines by the eye?

Beak Shape: Beak shape varies by what the bird eats. Nuthatches need thin, sharp beaks to tap into and pull insects out from the bark of a tree. Finches use their thick, cone shaped beaks for cracking seeds.

 Drilling (Woodpeckers)

 Catching Insects (Warblers, Nuthatches and Flycatchers)

 Sipping Nectar (Hummingbirds)

 Ripping (Eagles, Hawks and Vultures)

 Seed Cracking (Finches, Grosbeaks and Chickadees)

Tail Shape: Is the tail rounded like a jay's? Is it pointed like a mourning dove's? Or, is it notched like a goldfinch's?

Location: When not on a feeder, is the bird found on the ground, in bushes or trees or all three?

 Ground

 Bush

 Tree

Some birds, like goldfinches, are rarely seen on the ground while other birds, such as robins, are often seen on the ground looking for worms in the soil.

In this book, you will see pictures showing where you will find the bird, like this one from the American Robin page:

Look Here

Over time, you will find yourself using size and shape features more and more. You'll find yourself thinking.... is the beak more like the thick, powerful beak of a finch or more like the slender beak of a nuthatch?

Does the body shape look more like a nuthatch or a chickadee? Is it closer to the size of a robin or a crow? These new tools will help you get an impression of the bird more quickly. This is what birders call the bird's GISS (pronounced JIZZ): "General Impression of Size and Shape." And speed is a good thing in the birding world!

Once you have identified your bird, don't forget to add it to the '**My Awesome Backyard Bird List**' at the back of this book. It is always fun to look back at your list and see when and where you first saw a bird.

🎵 Bird Songs 🎵

All birds have a song or call. Many birds have more than one, but there is one call they use more than any other. Every time you hear a bird, try to find it. Getting to know a bird's song can be helpful in identifying the bird. It will also let you know when a new bird is singing in your yard because it is a bird whose song you do not know.

You may already know some birds' songs. For example, you probably hear the Black-capped Chickadee quite often ('*chick-a-dee-dee-dee*'). If you are lucky enough to have a Northern Cardinal nesting in your yard, you likely hear its loud '*peer, peer, peer*' call many times a day, often as soon as light comes into the sky in the morning. There's two already!

On each page of this book, you will find a QR code. Scanning the code with a phone or other device will take you to a web page where you can hear the bird's song. Be sure to get a grown-up's permission to do this.

When you have gained some practice with the birds in your yard or at your feeder, try taking a parent and your new skills on a walk through your neighborhood or at a nearby nature trail. You will be surprised how your skills build quickly over time, and you will be thrilled by the growing number of birds you can identify from memory.

Song

Black-capped Chickadee

American Goldfinch

Spinus tristis

Yellow
Black
White

Female

Length

Favorite Food

Look Here

Song

Goldfinches are very talkative! You can often hear them chattering away at the tops of trees, especially in the morning and late afternoon. The males lose almost all of their intense yellow color in the winter but then quickly brighten up early in the spring.

Common Yellowthroat
Geothlypis trichas

Black
Black
White

Female

Length

Favorite Food

Look Here

Song

Sometimes called the 'bandit' warbler, the male Common Yellowthroat has a black mask across its face. This is a bird that likes to sing. Listen for its *'Witchity! Witchity Witchity!'* The Common Yellowthroat is most often found in areas with thick, tangled plants and shrubs.

Yellow Warbler

Setophaga petechia

Yellow
Black
Red

Female

Length

Favorite Food

Look Here

Song

A bright, buttery yellow color, the male Yellow Warbler is one of the easiest warblers to spot. Listen and look for him singing, 'Sweet, sweet, sweet. I'm so sweet!' from the tops of bushes and willow trees.

Pine Warbler

Setophaga pinus

Yellow
Black
White

Length

Favorite Food

Look Here

Song

The Pine Warbler got its name because it is rarely seen away from pine trees. It is the only warbler that eats large amounts of seeds. It finds these high in pine trees at the base of clumps of pine needles or at your feeder! Pine Warblers sound a lot like Dark-eyed Juncos and Chipping Sparrows.

Baltimore Oriole

Icterus galbula

Orange
Black
White

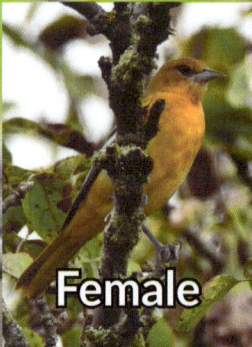

Female

Length

Baltimore Orioles are large, bright birds. They are similar to a robin, but the males are much brighter. It is hard to miss their orange bellies! They have a musical song and are often found at the tops or upper parts of trees looking for insects. However, they are easily tempted to feeders with orange slices or grape jelly.

Look Here

Favorite Food

Song

Red-eyed Vireo

Vireo olivaceus

Green
White
Red

Length

Favorite Food

Look Here

Song

The Red-eyed Vireo loves to sing! In fact, a male may sing up to 20,000 times in one day! Red-eyed Vireos are often found plucking caterpillars from leaves in treetops. The Red-eyed Vireo's eye does not turn red until the end of its first winter.

Ruby-throated Hummingbird
Archilochus colubris

Green
White
Red

Favorite Food

Male

Look Here

Length

Song

Female

Ruby-throated Hummingbirds are not shy. They will hover and feed from hanging plants and flowers in your garden, especially those flowers that are red or orange. The Ruby-throated Hummingbird beats its wings about 53 times a second. Listen closely, and you will hear the buzz of their wings as they zip past you!

Eastern Phoebe

Sayornis phoebe

Gray
White
Brown

Length

Favorite Food

Look Here

Song

This is a bird who will sing its name 'Phoebe!' over and over again. A type of flycatcher, it will dart from its perch, grab an insect mid-air, and return to its perch to enjoy its meal. When perched, the Eastern Phoebe sits upright and wags its tail almost constantly.

Tufted Titmouse

Baeolophus bicolor

Gray
White
Orange

Length

Favorite Food

Look Here

Song

If you hear a bird singing *'Peter! Peter! Peter!'*, it is a Tufted Titmouse. With its bold black eye and crest of gray atop its head, the Tufted Titmouse loves to come to feeders. Watch it grab a seed and take it to a nearby perch where it will crack the seed open and enjoy a tasty treat!

White-breasted Nuthatch
Sitta carolinensis

Gray
White
Black

Length

Favorite Food

Look Here

Song

Nuthatches got their name because they like to jam large nuts and acorns into tree bark, then whack them with their sharp bills to "hatch" out the seed from the inside. Like the Red-breasted Nuthatch, a White-breasted will climb headfirst down tree trunks.

Red-breasted Nuthatch
Sitta canadensis

Gray
White
Red

Length

Favorite Food

Look Here

Song

Mostly seen in winter, this tiny nuthatch is often found climbing headfirst down tree trunks probing for the insects it likes to eat. Its 'Yank! Yank!' call sounds like a tiny horn.

Common Redpoll

Acanthis flammea

Gray
Red
Black

Female

Length

Favorite Food

Look Here

Song

Common Redpolls are active birds that often travel in flocks. Although more often seen in the Arctic and the forests of Canada, they can be seen in New England in the winter. Common Redpolls are smart birds and will make tunnels in the snow to stay warm during the night!

Mourning Dove
Zenaida macroura

Gray
Brown
Black

Song

Female

Favorite Food

Look Here

Length

Male

The *'Coo'* of the pigeon-like Mourning Dove is often mistaken for an owl. When it flies, its wings make a sharp whistling sound or a whinnying sound like a horse. Mourning Doves can often be found perched on power lines or looking for seeds on the ground.

Gray Catbird

Dumetella carolinensis

Gray
Black

Length

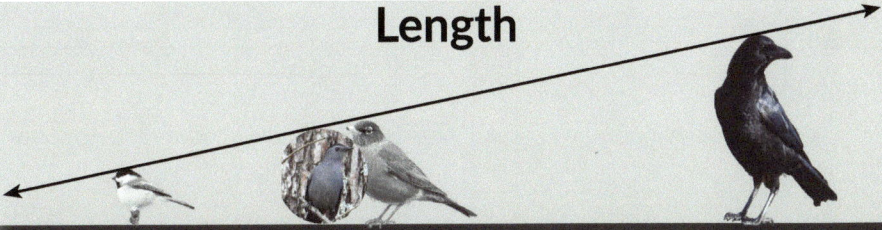

Favorite Food

Look Here

Song

The Gray Catbird is named for the loud '*Meow!*' call it gives when disturbed or at the end of its song. Like the Northern Mockingbird, the Gray Catbird mimics, or copies, the songs of other birds and includes a variety of them in its own song. A catbird may sing for up to 10 minutes!

Northern Mockingbird

Mimus polyglottos

Gray
Black
Orange

Song

Length

Favorite Food

Look Here

The Northern Mockingbird earned its name for its habit of mimicking, or mocking, the songs of other birds. It repeats each of those songs three or more times when it sings. The mockingbird is always learning new songs from other birds. A male may learn up to 200 new songs during his life!

In flight, the Northern Mockingbird shows bold white patches on its wings and its outer tail feathers.

Red-bellied Woodpecker

Melanerpes carolinus

Gray
Black
Red

Female

Length

Favorite Food

Look Here

Song

Don't try to find the red belly on the Red-bellied Woodpecker. It is almost invisible! Instead, it has a long patch of red on the back of its head extending from the crown, or top, to the neck. In the male, the red patch goes all the way to the forehead.

Rock Pigeon
Accelleratti Incredibus

Gray
Green
Orange

Female

Length

Favorite Food

Look Here

Song

Rock Pigeons love to live near people and are usually found near buildings. Pigeons bob their heads back and forth as they walk to help keep their vision focused on what is around them.

Northern Cardinal

Cardinalis cardinalis

Red
Black

Female

Length

Favorite Food

Look Here

Song

The Northern Cardinal keeps its colors year-round, making the bright red males really stand out against the snow in a New England winter. Male and female cardinal couples are almost always together. If you see one, look for the other. You will find him or her nearby. Cardinals are often the first birds to sing in the morning.

House Finch

Haemorhous mexicanus

Red
Brown
White

Female

Length

Favorite Food

Look Here

Song

House Finches have a very musical song and love to come to feeders. Look for the bright red head of the male. If you have hanging plants at your house, keep a close watch on them in the spring. A pair of house finches might build a nest in one!

American Robin

Turdus migratorius

Red
Black
White

Favorite Food

Look Here

Length

Song

People think of robins as being signs of spring. Actually, many robins do not migrate, or leave, New England in the winter. Instead, they will stay year-round. Robins can often be seen searching for earthworms in lawns after a rain storm as the worms come to the surface in search of water.

Song Sparrow

Melospiza melodia

Brown
White
Black

Length

Favorite Food

Look Here

Song

As its name suggests, this bird loves to sing! If you see a small brown bird with lots of streaks on its chest perched on a shrub with its head tilted back and singing, it is most likely the Song Sparrow!

White-throated Sparrow

Zonotrichia albicollis

Brown
White
Yellow

Female

Length

Favorite Food

Look Here

Song

White-throated Sparrows feed mainly on the ground under bushes or at the woods' edge. They are often found in flocks and sing loudly the name of their breeding grounds, '*Oh, sweet Canada! Canada! Canada!*'

House Wren

Troglodytes aedon

Brown
Orange
Gray

Length

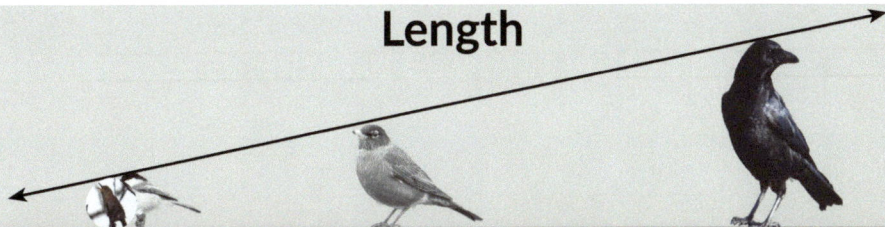

Favorite Food

Look Here

Song

House Wrens are little birds that fly quickly from shrubs and low branches to snatch insects from the air. The male house wren builds several nest foundations for the female to choose from. When she finds the one she likes best, she adds the final lining.

Chipping Sparrow
Spizella passerina

Brown
Gray
Red

Length

Favorite Food

Look Here

Song

If you see a little bird feeding on the ground near the edge of a road, look to see if it has a cinnamon colored cap. If so, you have found a Chipping Sparrow! Chipping Sparrows are also commonly found in backyards where they will come to feeders or eat seed spilled on the ground.

Northern Flicker

Colaptes auratus

Brown
Black
Red

Length

Favorite Food

Look Here

Song

Northern Flickers act differently than other woodpeckers. You are more likely to find them on the ground where their favorite foods (ants and beetles) are than in trees. When it flies, it shows yellow under its wings and a bright patch of white on its rump, where the back connects to the tail.

Female

Length

Favorite Food

Look Here

Song

Brown-headed Cowbirds are lazy parents! Instead of building nests themselves, they lay their eggs in the nests of other birds and leave. They hope that the other bird parents will take care of their babies too.

Carolina Wren

Thryothorus ludovicianus

Brown
Black
White

Length

Favorite Food

Look Here

Song

Unlike many species of birds who sing only during breeding season, the male Carolina Wren can be heard singing at any time of year. It is a shy bird with a size much smaller than its loud *'Teakettle! Teakettle!'* song suggests.

House Sparrow

Passer domesticus

Brown
Black
White

Female

Length

Favorite Food

Look Here

Song

House Sparrows are rarely found in places where there are not houses or other buildings. They are sometimes called the English Sparrow because they were first brought here from England.

Blue Jay
Cyanocitta cristata

Blue
White
Black

Song

Look Here

Length

Favorite Food

Blue Jays are aggressive and will chase other birds away from feeders. They are also quite loud and will mimic other birds, even hawks!

Eastern Bluebird

Sialia sialis

Blue
Orange
White

Male

Female

Length

Favorite Food

Look Here

Song

If you spot a flash of bright blue, you might be seeing a male Eastern Bluebird! When not flying, they can often be seen sitting on power lines, nest boxes or fences.

Black-capped Chickadee
Poecile atricapillus

Black
White
Brown

Favorite Food

Look Here

The Black-capped Chickadee is a year-round resident of New England. They are quite tame. Many people have been able to get chickadees to eat seeds right from their hands!

Length

Song

Downy Woodpecker

Dryobates pubescens

Black
White
Red

Female

Song

Like the Hairy Woodpecker, the active Downy Woodpecker makes round holes in trees when drilling the bark in search of insects. A good way to tell it apart from the very similar Hairy Woodpecker is by the size of its beak. It is about half as long as its head.

Length

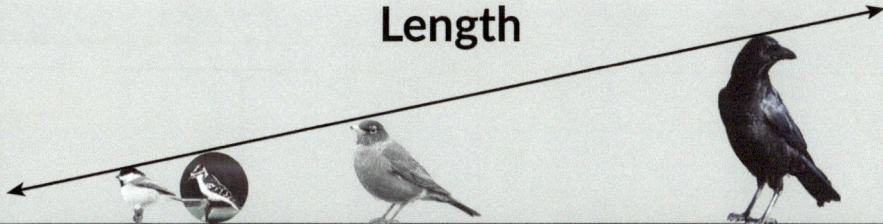

Male

Favorite Food

Look Here

European Starling

Sturnus vulgaris

Black
White
Yellow

Length

Favorite Food

Look Here

Song

The European Starling is usually seen traveling in large, noisy flocks. They often land on lawns before suddenly taking off again. Covered in white spots in the winter, starlings turn dark and glossy in summer.

Hairy Woodpecker
Dryobates villosus

Black
White
Red

Female

Length

Favorite Food

Look Here

Song

Like the Downy Woodpecker, the Hairy Woodpecker makes round holes in trees when drilling the bark in search of insects. A good way to tell it apart from the very similar Downy Woodpecker is by the size of its beak. It is almost as long as its head. It also holds its head quite straight and high, like a soldier.

Yellow-rumped Warbler
Steophaga coronata

Black
Yellow
White

Female

Length

Favorite Food

Look Here

Song

Yellow-rumped Warblers like to perch on outer branches of trees from where they zip out to catch insects. Look for the flash of yellow on their rumps as they fly. That yellow rump flash is how they got the nickname, 'butter butt'!

Dark-eyed Junco

Accelleratti Incredibus

Favorite Food

Look Here

When they fly, Dark-eyed Juncos show a flash of white along their outer tail feathers. They often travel in flocks and will come to feeders and also feed on the ground underneath them. They are one of the most abundant forest birds in North America.

Length

Female

Song

Pileated Woodpecker
Dryocopus pileatus

Blue
Red
White

Length

Favorite Food

Look Here

Song

Almost as large as a crow, the Pileated Woodpecker whacks large rectangular holes into trees in search of carpenter ants. Other birds, such as swifts, ducks and owls will make homes in the holes. The Pileated Woodpecker looks prehistoric, somewhat like a Pterodactyl!

Wild Turkey
Accelleratti Incredibus

Black
Red
Blue

Females

Length

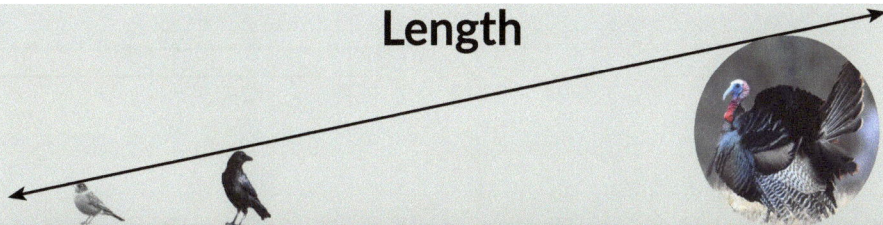

Favorite Food

Look Here

Song

Wild Turkeys can swim when they need to by tucking their wings in close, spreading their tails, and kicking.

Turkey fossils have been unearthed across the southern United States and Mexico, some of them dating from more than 5 million years ago.

Red-winged Blackbird
Agelaius phoeniceus

Black
Red
Yellow

Song

Favorite Food

Look Here

Length

Female

Often found in wet areas where cattails are, Red-winged Blackbirds will also come to your feeder. They prefer to feed on the ground, so look for them eating seeds that other birds have dropped or that you have scattered there.

Common Grackle

Quiscalus quiscula

Black
Blue
Yellow

Female

Length

Favorite Food

Look Here

Song

In the shade, a Common Grackle looks a lot like a crow. In the sun, their heads are a shiny blue-green, and their tails and wings show a deep purple tint. Notice their bright yellow eyes. They can look a little scary!

American Crow

Black

Corvus brachyhynchos

Song

Look Here

Length

Favorite Food

American Crows are one of the smartest birds. They even make tools. They can shape a twig into a hook to spear a slug! Crows will gather in large groups in trees in the evening to 'roost', or sleep.

My Awesome Backyard Bird List

	Bird Name	Date Seen	Observations
☑	American Crow (example)	July 29	Eating Seeds
☐	American Crow		
☐	American Goldfinch		
☐	American Robin		
☐	Baltimore Oriole		
☐	Black-capped Chickadee		
☐	Blue Jay		
☐	Brown-headed Cowbird		
☐	Carolina Wren		
☐	Chipping Sparrow		
☐	Common Grackle		
☐	Common Redpoll		
☐	Common Yellowthroat		

	Bird Name	Date Seen	Observations
☐	Dark-eyed Junco		
☐	Downy Woodpecker		
☐	Eastern Bluebird		
☐	Eastern Phoebe		
☐	European Starlings		
☐	Gray Catbird		
☐	Hairy Woodpecker		
☐	House Finch		
☐	House Sparrow		
☐	House Wren		
☐	Mourning Dove		
☐	Northern Cardinal		
☐	Northern Flicker		
☐	Northern Mockingbird		

	Bird Name	Date Seen	Observations
☐	Pileated Woodpecker		
☐	Pine Warbler		
☐	Red-bellied Woodpecker		
☐	Red-breasted Nuthatch		
☐	Red-eyed Vireo		
☐	Red-winged Blackbird		
☐	Rock Pigeon		
☐	Ruby-throated Hummingbird		
☐	Song Sparrow		
☐	Tufted Titmouse		
☐	White-breasted Nuthatch		
☐	White-throated Sparrow		
☐	Wild Turkey		
☐	Yellow Warbler		

	Bird Name	Date Seen	Observations
☐	Yellow-rumped Warbler		
☐			
☐			
☐			
☐			
☐			
☐			
☐			
☐			
☐			
☐			
☐			
☐			
☐			
☐			
☐			

Attracting and Seeing Birds

If you want to see birds more closely, you can do two things - put bird feeders in your yard and use a pair of binoculars.

Bird Feeders

There are many different kinds of bird feeders you can find at bird feeding stores, gift shops, hardware stores and department stores. Almost any store that sells birdseed will also have bird feeders.

While you can certainly use store bought feeders, you can also make your own bird feeder using items commonly found around the house or yard.

DIY (Do It Yourself) Bird Feeders to Make at Home

Here are three bird feeder projects you can make at home. Be sure to get an adult to help with any poking or cutting steps in your chosen project.

Pine Cone Bird Feeder

Materials:

- One Pine Cone
- Peanut Butter or other Nut Butter
- 12" of Yarn, Twine, or Fishing Line
- Birdseed

- Wax Paper or Newspaper for covering your work surface

Steps:

1. Spread the wax paper on your work surface.
2. Tie the yarn around the top of the pine cone, making a loop for hanging.

3. Using a spoon or knife, spread peanut butter on the pine cone. Try to fill in as many spaces as possible.

4. Carefully pour some birdseed on the wax paper.

5. Roll the peanut butter-covered pine cone in the bird-seed.
6. Gently tap the pine cone to get off loose birdseed.

7. Hang your bird feeder from a tree or shrub branch.

8. Start watching for birds to come and feast!

Bread Slice Bird Feeder

Materials:

- One Slice of Stale Bread (be sure the bread has dried out completely)
- Peanut Butter or other Nut Butter
- 12" of string, wire or a long twist-tie
- Birdseed

Steps:

1. Spread the wax paper on your work surface.
2. Poke a hole through the bread near the top (leave enough bread at the top so that the string will not pull through) and thread the twist-tie or string through and close to make a loop.

3. Spread peanut butter on one or both sides of the bread.

4. Put birdseed on a plate and dip one side of the bread. into the seed, pressing lightly. Repeat with the other

side if making your feeder two-sided.

5. Attach to a sturdy branch in your backyard.

6. Watch birds come to your new feeder!

Soda Bottle Bird Feeder

Be sure to get the help of an adult for the cutting steps in this project.

- Materials:
- 2-liter plastic bottle
- Twine or wire
- 1 Pencil or Chopstick
- Scissors or a knife
- Duct tape
- Funnel
- Birdseed

1. Remove all labels from the soda bottle and wash. Save the cap. Dry the outside of the bottle with a towel.
2. **A grown-up MUST do this step.** Turn the bottle over.

Using scissors, poke two small holes in the bottom of the bottle or on the sides close to the bottom.

3. Thread twine or wire through one hole and out the other. Loosely tie the twine or wire together to make a loop for hanging. The bottom of the bottle will become the top of the feeder.

4. **A grown-up MUST do this step.** Cut or poke two holes on opposite sides of the bottle, three inches from the bottle cap. Make the holes just large enough for a pencil (or chopstick) to fit through.
5. Insert the pencil or chopstick through the holes. This will make a perch for the birds to sit on.

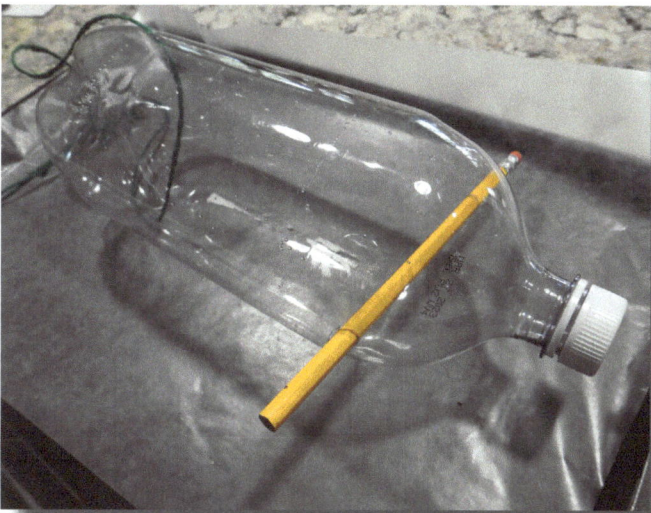

6. **A grown-up MUST do this step.** Cut or poke ⅓ inch holes two inches above each perch. This is where the

birds will get the seed. Depending on the size of the birdseed you plan to use, you may need to make the holes bigger.

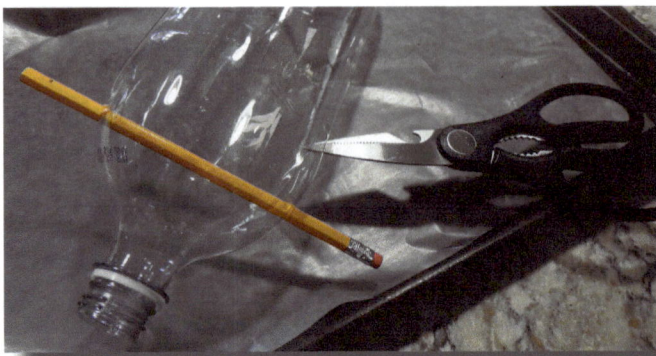

7. Turn the bottle right-side up. Using a funnel, carefully fill the bottle halfway with birdseed.

8. Screw the cap onto the bottle. Add duct tape around the cap if needed.
9. Turn the bottle over. Hang the twine or wire around a tree limb or hang outside a window. Watch the birds

come to your feeder!

The simplest of all feeders is to sprinkle seed on the ground or a deck railing and watch who comes to eat!

Types of Birdseed

Just like there are many different birds, there are also many different types of birdseed. Some of the most common and easy to find in supermarkets and hardware stores are:

Black Oil Sunflower Seed
If you have just one feeder, this is the seed to fill it with. Black oil sunflower seed attracts a wide variety of birds. They love it!

Thistle Seed (also known as Nyjer)

Finches of all kinds love this seed. While special feeders are made just to hold thistle seed, you can put it in a platform or hutch feeder as well.

Mixed Seed

Unsure of what to get? You can't go wrong with a mix of seed. There are many different blends of mixed seed. The bag will tell you which birds are mostly likely to come to the feeder for it.

Suet Cakes

Suet is a fat-based bird feeding product. It is most commonly sold in 'cakes' and is placed in a special wire holder either hung from a tree or attached to a pole or other bird feeder. Suet is a favorite of woodpeckers, but many other birds like it as well. During the winter, migration and breeding season when birds need to eat a lot, suet is an excellent source of energy.

Binoculars

Binoculars come in a variety of sizes and some are very expensive. But you don't need an expensive pair of binoculars to be able to get a much better view of a bird than you can get with your eyes alone. In fact, there are binoculars made especially for kids and for people who want try out using binoculars but don't want to spend a lot of money. A visit to your local bird feeding store, Audubon Society chapter, or a search on an on-line store can help you find just the right pair for you.

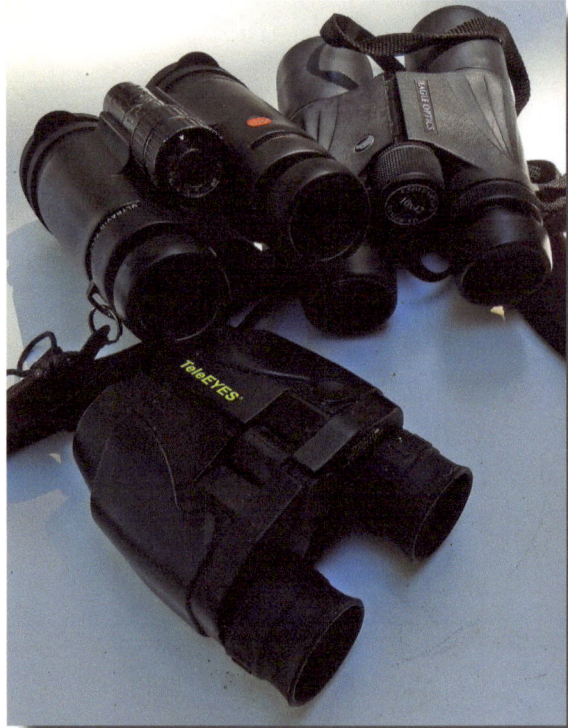

About the Authors

Ingrid and Ethan Whitaker are experienced birders who bring their professional experience to their hobby and to this book.

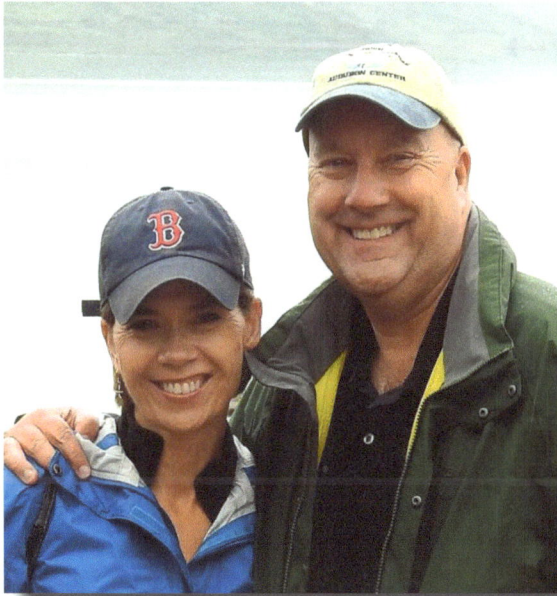

Ingrid is an award winning teacher (recipient of the Presidential Award for Excellence in Science Teaching and Maine Teacher of the Year Finalist). She has thirty plus years in the classroom where she has educated and inspired hundreds of young people.

Ethan is a retired software developer and entrepreneur who has started and sold multiple companies.

In 2021, Ethan broke Maine's Big Year Birding record, finding and identifying 324 species of birds in the State in a single calendar year.

Ethan and Ingrid wrote about their Big Year Adventure, in "Every Bird in Maine", available where Birding Books are sold.

BY ETHAN WHITAKER

ONE MAN'S JOURNEY TO SEE
EVERY BIRD IN MAINE

Index

Red-winged Blackbir